HellHound

7 Leadership Styles Explained in Doggy Terms

Tyra Hodge Ph.D.

Hodge Publishing Books by
Tyra Hodge Ph.D.

Out of the Ashes ~ A Wounded
Daughters Diary

God's Plan for Black America

Don't Date Him~ A Guide to Not
Dating the Wrong Man

DEDICATION

I believe that my Heavenly Father gave me the inspiration for this book. I dedicate this book to Him and ask Him to bless the things I've learned throughout the years in hopes that I can lead other leaders into finding the greatness hidden within themselves.

Contents

Preface

Leaders are mostly natural-born creatures. Some leaders are cultivated in time; however, natural-born leaders will most likely find their place in life in whatever career they choose. John C. Maxwell, one of the world's twenty-first century authorities on leadership, states, "A successful person finds the right place for himself. But a successful leader finds the right place for others."

Most times, these natural leaders will develop and grow within their calling because of their attention to their craft and their career timing.

More importantly, an effective leader will instinctively embrace the talents and skills of others that will, in turn, strengthen their own leadership abilities.

For years, as a public-school teacher and child behaviorist, I observed the natural-born leaders who emerged within my classroom context, noticing the different styles of these leaders as they jockeyed for their position. Some had good instincts for being a positive influence among their fellow classmates, while others exhibited more negative behaviors through aggressive bullying and deceptive influences.

As I studied my students' behaviors, I also carefully took mental notes of the professional leadership styles and personalities of other teachers and administrators who worked with me in education. Interestingly, through my many observations, I discovered that my young students and the adults within my leadership team reflected similar leadership styles and personality traits. The students reflected a slightly more immature version of their adult counterparts in style, but I identified distinctive and similar positive and negative influential leadership types within both groups. As I continued to note these observations about people within my industry, I also began to draw conclusions about their behavior compared to other species.

As I developed my theories about leadership styles among my students and adult leadership teams, I began to connect these same styles to the canine social hierarchy. Besides the fact that I love dogs, watching these amazing animals operate within their natural setting in my earlier years helped shape my awareness and understanding of behavior in general. As a people watcher and a dog watcher, it became evident to me that there are many similarities in the way the two species are structured for leadership styles.

From my natural curiosity of behaviors in people and canines, I gained a deeper awareness of both species' hierarchy of leadership traits that led to the formulation of this leadership guide in 'doggy language.'

My goal is to help build better leaders and more efficient teams that can exist within any organization. Additionally, my hope is that leaders will better understand their personal influence over their teams by more clearly viewing the pros and cons of their leadership style through the lens of a dog.

Introduction

Teamwork goes hand in hand with leadership and understanding the personalities that make up an effective team is crucial to good team leadership. Leaders do not always have the luxury of choosing their followers, and it is even rarer that followers are in the situation to choose their leaders. When a team is not acting cohesively, I believe it is the leader's responsibility to make appropriate leadership style changes to bring about progress.

A talented, influential, and responsible leader that is self-aware understands the talents and abilities that exist within their social hierarchy and makes the appropriate adjustments to their style of leadership, which in turn can save a sinking ship or change its direction to a positive one.

God purposely made many different distinctive personalities and leadership styles among his creation of beings. Each personality type within a team has its necessary function. It is the responsibility of a good leader to understand the specific strengths and weaknesses of its members and determine how to influence each one to provide their best work for the team.

A good leader understands and cares for his followers, and with this kind of synergy working in a team environment, the followers will go to the ends of the earth for the good leader, whether they are human or canine. I can think back to one of my class's favorite books, *The Call of the Wild* by Jack London, where the protagonist, a caring and trusted dog named Buck, proved to be an excellent dog pack leader.

Once he took charge of his pack, he influenced them to turn from acting like an unruly team of dogs to a cooperative and productive team. The pack's strict purpose was to ensure the Canadian Government's mail was delivered promptly despite the difficult weather conditions and long distances the sled dogs were to travel. By keeping order among the dogs, doing his fair share of the work, and caring for each of the pack members, the team worked the hardest to ensure they met their goal for each delivery.

The slick manner in which Buck was able to obtain the pack's loyalty and trust speaks of his positive influence over the group and influence he began to develop from the first moment he was locked into the sled traces as a rookie sled dog with other dogs he barely knew.

At the beginning of his career as a rookie sled dog, Buck was placed between two long-term career dogs, Dave and Sol-leks, to learn the way of the team. He humbled himself and waited for his leadership opportunity to present itself. Buck was the one dynamic character in the story that learned to adapt to his environment and circumstance. Initially, he learned how *not* to be a leader as he watched his original pack leader, Spitz, bully his way with the team. Spitz sometimes acted friendly to the team but could not be trusted as he stole food and tricked the other dogs for purely selfish reasons. He was not respected and developed very little influence over his team.

In this story, Jack London also provides examples of poor human leadership by providing excerpts of cruelty over the pack dogs by the men mushers or sled masters. There were times these men used brute force to make the dogs submit and work hard, but it was evident the dogs grew to resent these leaders and would turn on them when pushed too hard as they learned their leader could not be trusted.

John C. Maxwell states in one of his best books, *The 21 Indispensable Qualities of a Leader*, that "Trust is the foundation of leadership, and it is the most important asset of a leader." Maxwell also says three qualities a leader must exemplify to build trust are competence, connection, and character.

When Spitz didn't build trust in the pack because of his constant display of incompetence, the pack turned against him, allowing Buck to usurp Spitz's leadership. When the sled master beat and starved the dogs as punishment, the dogs resented him for his cruelty and expressed their anger with growling, biting, and the display of their fangs, transforming any sense of loyalty they once had for him to distrust and hatred. Sometimes, for their very survival, these consistent cruel acts from their musher would alter the true personalities of the dogs, causing them to lose their confidence, and bully and lash out at the other dogs.

Whether human or canine, when a leader loses influence amongst his team members, it is usually because the leader is not investing in the team and not demonstrating appropriate care and connection with them. As John Maxwell says, "When people respect you as a person, they admire you. When they respect you as a friend, they love you. When they respect you as a leader, they follow you."

The Seven Different Dog Personalities

These are documented dog personalities that resemble the leadership styles I have observed in dog packs. The American Kennel Club states that there are personalities unique to the dog and not to the breed. In March 1979, the American Kennel Club *Gazette* compiled seven general dog personalities. Their names and descriptive summaries are based on the *Gazette's* article. I also provided a corresponding canine leadership style, names that I assigned each type based on my association with these workplace personalities.

Aggressive or Hellhound: This type of dog can be considered a leader but does not necessarily display the best leadership characteristics. This personality demonstrates extreme dominance and can easily be provoked into biting. The dominant nature of this dog allows him to resist human leadership, requiring strict guidance and a consistent but rigorous training program. Some Aggressive dogs were once a Confident-type dog that was mistreated and turned aggressive for self-protection. These dogs can be an excellent choice as a guard or police dog.

Narcissist or Hyena: This type of dog is a grunt worker. He never sees the good in others, and he constantly undermines the efforts of everybody else. The Hyena dog is never satisfied by any path the leader chooses to find food and always seems to have a better alternative. As a leader, the Hyena is super arrogant and trashes the opinion of his followers if they contradict his in the slightest. He rebels against his human owner and will constantly show signs of disloyalty. They are usually very strong-willed and will do anything to show that their ideas are the best. This usually leads to undisputed success; however, at the most difficult possible route.

Confident or Super Alpha: This dog type is dominant and self-assured but can be provoked to bite. However, the Confident dog readily accepts human leadership that is firm and consistent. This dog responds best to an owner that is determined and decisive and, in the right hands, the Confident dog can be a fine working or show dog. With an owner that knows how to guide this dog using consistency, the Confident dog can be a family's form of protection.

Outgoing or Alpha: A dog with this type of personality is friendly and pleasant. He will be well adjusted if he receives an outlet for his energy with regular training and exercise. Outgoing-type dogs have a flexible temperament that adapts well to different types of en-

18

vironments, provided he is not treated harshly. They can be excellent family pets in the right type of household.

Adaptable or Beta: This dog is easy to handle and quite cooperative. Their submissive nature will have them continually look to their master for leadership. This dog is easy to train, reliable with children, and though he lacks self-confidence, he makes a high-quality family pet. He is usually less extroverted with a demeanor that is gentle and affectionate.

Insecure or Omega: This dog is extremely submissive and lacks self-confidence. It closely bonds with its owner and requires regular companionship with lots of encouragement. If this dog type is treated too harshly, it will be very shy and fearful. It will do best in a predictable and structured environment with an owner who is patient and willing to allow the dog some time and grace to emerge from his shyness.

Independent or Delta: A dog with an independent personality is uninterested in people. It will mature into a not affectionate dog and will have a low need for human companionship. To perform as intended, these dogs require a purposeful job that is not compromised by strong attachments to their owner.

1

Hellhound

God help the person that crosses the Hellhound! The name says it all. They can be natural-born leaders but not always. Their leadership may either be stolen by underhand means, burning someone else, or clawing their way to the top; most of the time, they are placed in leadership before they are ready to lead.

The Hellhound does not like having people around but keeps people around as ornamental displays. They need to run the show and have someone to boss around. This person loves to dish out punitive justice in front of others to see how strong and powerful they are. This person has few boundaries and is constantly into other people's business. They have much-assumed power and lead with an iron fist. When they crash and burn, they will likely burn their organization to the ground.

Hellhounds run their position like an evil dictator. They have difficulty acknowledging the good qualities in others. They rarely give credit where credit is due, and if they do acknowledge a positive, it is followed with a hard *but*. The bottom line is that they are bullies, and these leader types will steal your job if you let them.

In the beginning, a new person to the organization is never welcomed by a Hellhound. The rookie will sometimes need to watch out for an act of sabotage and bullying behaviors from the Hellhounds. I am not certain if the Hellhound really likes people because they rarely seem interested in the ideas from other team members.

The Hellhound can be a man or woman. This person tends to be abusive in their personal life and/or has been abused by someone in the past. If the Hellhound has supporters, they exist to constantly affirm the greatness of their leader. However, if their supporters ever display a different way of thinking, then they are quickly and openly shamed before they are put back in their place of servitude.

The Hellhound is not always born a Hellhound. A traumatic life event, a new power position, or major stressor in their life can change a good leader into a Hellhound. A Hellhound will push their way to the spotlight. They sometimes have trouble delegating but will complain that no one else is doing their part. The Hellhound sees friendly differences as a battlefield. They tend to talk over others to win an agreement but may still be completely wrong. If they are found to be wrong, they have difficulty accepting the truth. They micromanage their team members, which may increase productivity for a short time, but will usually generate a high turnover rate causing a low staff retention level.

This leader has an allegiance to no one but themselves. They thrive on the intrinsic rewards from their accomplishments and in the subduing of others. The only way I have found to restore the humanity of a Hellhound is either to remove them from their leadership position or to stage a coup that requires them to reflect on the grievances expressed by their team members.

Having a Hellhound as a leader can prove to be useful when needing a headhunter or someone that can win a position for your benefit. Hellhounds are also valuable when an organization needs to restructure, where the old leadership is removed, and new leadership is installed. The Hellhound's gift to uproot undesirable employees is remarkable. This person typically will enter a large organization, remove the existing key people, and replace them with their own support systems who are mostly inadequate minions.

If the job of the Hellhound is to restructure an organization and then to move on to the next job, then this person has found their calling. The Hellhound will understand where the key people are needed. They will know how to uproot and replace quickly so an organization can be turned around to greatness. Their intrinsic reward for this is that they successfully restructured a company and made it great, and then moved on to repeat their cycle.

Stories of the Hellhound

I have worked under three Hellhounds in my work experience. The first was when I was young in teaching. I quickly rose to leadership in a behavioral specialist position. My supervisor was knowledgeable in her field of education. If my memory serves me correctly, this supervisor was effective until she had a traumatic event in her life. Afterward, she changed for the worse, lasting in her position for approximately two years.

I admit she performed some crazy antics during the time of our work experience. For instance, I watched how she twisted the words of people who she did not like. If anyone was publicly complimented, she made it a point to contradict the person's character being admired. I personally witnessed this supervisor refusing to give positive job references for team members I knew to be deserving. Twice, her actions were against colleagues for whom I had inside information. Once, I felt it was my duty to exchange one recommendation she gave with my own recommendation because I personally supervised and knew the excellent qualities and work ethic of the person in question. Additionally, when discussing students with this Hellhound, it was always important for her to know whether the student was black or white. It seemed she had serious racial biases, impairing her ability to view students equally.

After about two years of working with this person, a coup was staged against her, and a list of grievances was detailed against her. It was at this time that I learned this woman had given false information about my character and abilities to anyone in leadership that would listen. Someone was nice enough to share the information that she was circulating. I knew a promotion would become unlikely, and I secretly applied to leave the job. When it was uncovered that she was blocking my attempts to leave, I went back to my former employer, and they were ecstatic to help me.

After a month, I ran into the old employer, and she dared to ask me why I did not use her for a reference. This was a very odd question coming from someone that sought to ruin my reputation. So, I decided to answer her question; my response was, "I did not use you as a reference because I wanted the job."

There was another Hellhound that I worked for; let's just call her Marsha. Marsha was the principal of a school where I decided to work as a behavior specialist. Marsha was very clear about the standards that she wanted me to keep and that she had had a bad experience with the former employee. Marsha was very excited about me joining the team because I was a highly sought-after behavior specialist.

Marsha repeatedly bragged about my talents and what she had heard about me, but unknown to me, the school already had a behavior specialist. This did not make the other behavior specialist happy, especially when Marsha kept bragging about me. This particular year I had to come up against two different types of battles—one with the supervisor and the other with the jealous co-worker.

On the one hand, I had a co-worker that was constantly criticizing my paperwork. Because the principal really didn't know a lot about this special education paperwork, she instinctively believed the co-worker. Don't forget that I was hand-trained by district specialists who was trained by the state's regional service centers. So, I did my job to the best of my ability, and I produced results with the students.

A few times I was to exit a student from a behavioral program, which was a huge deal, the co-worker would take that student from me and put them in her program so she would get the credit for their exit. This co-worker continued to downplay my work to my supervisor. The difference between the co-worker and me was that she was senior staff, and she did produce results, but she used bullying as one of her main ways of working. I find this counterproductive when working with students with serious behavior problems. This just teaches them that they may not be able to bully you, but they learn how to bully better.

So this co-worker proved to be a bully and used her position to have the principal bully me. There were times that I would walk in and find my supervisor digging through my computer looking for evidence of corruption, searching my desk, and calling my paperwork crap when in fact, she never even read it. There is one thing that a good behavior specialist has going for them; there is always another job out there because not many people want to do what we do. So, I decided that my first year there would be my last year and I went somewhere with a better work environment.

This is how I see working with Hellhounds, although we have a choice in where we work, and if you're good at your job, then your gift will make room for you. I have had people want to work with me so badly they were willing to reorganize and raise their whole faculty and staff to have me work with their students. I understand being comfortable in a place, feeling like you can't go anywhere else, but the fact is you can. If you are being abused mentally at work, you do not have to stay. Abuse doesn't just happen at home and behind closed doors to children and women. Abuse can happen at work. And you don't have to take it; if you are good at your job, find another one. In working with Marsha, I did resign from my job to find another place to work; the next year they were looking for me and wanting me back, so apparently the job that I did wasn't so crappy. The person that they hired to replace me could not handle it and quit. The co-worker who gave me such a hard time did not even stay at the job—she went on to make somebody else miserable. And she did not even last at the next job she had. I don't find any joy in anybody's suffering or failures because I realize that I am responsible for my God. I am responsible for my family, and I am responsible for myself.

The last Hellhound I'm going to tell you about was at a job I took in East Texas as a district behavior specialist. This was a new and exciting adventure because we were creating a special education department. This department consisted of about twenty new people connected to the Superintendent of the new development. There were three of us that weren't familiar with the Superintendent previously, but everyone else had already either known each other or were connected with the Superintendent or had gone to school with him. I guess this isn't a problem because it's very true sometimes when a person says that "it is not what you know, but it indeed, in fact, is about who you know."

Now, for the people that don't know anyone and got their job based on experience, know how this can be a difficult situation for them. This particular Hellhound was not the Superintendent; it was a co-worker within that group. This co-worker would always announce whenever she ran a behavior program that she would do it a particularly different way. She would say things like 'all the other behavior specialists I know do it this way.' That was fine because many ways on many roads can lead you to have successful students. I noticed with this particular person that any idea I had was usually contradicted by her openly and publicly, and I think friendly disagreements are good for growth. But there was one specific time that I was presenting to my team of workers that I was the head of, and this Hellhound was contradicting the research that I was presenting. She disrupted the meeting I was having with my subordinates; she even pulled out a book containing information that she was trying to use to contradict my teaching.

At one point, she even took the marker out of my hand and began teaching it to my group of subordinates. I saw the look of confusion on the people that worked under me. However, I was quite confused myself. I quietly sat down and allowed this person to continue teaching my staff development; I'd never yet encountered a person quite like that. If that example wasn't bad enough to make me look bad, this Hellhound went into documentation and changed students' data to reflect that I was not doing my job. What this person did not know was that the forms in Google record when a person changes data and who it was that changed it. So when I went to the Superintendent and told them that this person changed my student data and presented it as evidence of me not doing my job, the answer the Superintendent gave me was, "why would anybody go through that trouble to do something like that to you?"

I saw at that moment that the conversation with the Superintendent about my concerns would not be validated, and the lengths this person chose to go through to undervalue my services were not really worth continuing in a job that was highly stressful already. It is not easy when you work in a field of education where the students' behaviors are so extreme, and due to this, a person in my position must be trained to always remain calm.

So I had to decide whether this was a battle that I wanted to continue with this person in a group of people I was an outsider to. I did recognize that this person had worked for multiple districts, which was a red flag for me. I also notice how it was very important to this person to win arguments with the schools' principals in our district. I had to consider the lengths to which this person went to discredit the value that I brought to the district, and I had to decide if this was a battle that I wanted to continue to engage in or if it was something I was willing to give up.

At that particular point in my life, I was so close to graduating with one of my degrees, and I knew that I wanted to make more money anyway; I chose not to engage in a battle like that. I chose not to work with dishonest people that are willing to change data to win and that are willing to go behind people's backs just to make themselves look better.

You are probably saying, "Well, why didn't you stay and fight in some of these situations." Culture is very important when you're working in an organizational system. Culture can make a system successful, and culture can tear a system apart. Because I already work in a highly stressful and pressured area of education, the culture around me needs to be conducive to support that. For some people, this would have been the perfect place for them to work because they thrive on that type of drama; they live for fights like that. As a teacher or someone with the gift of teaching, they thrive on learning from mistakes, they thrive on being able to teach and see the fruits of their teaching, but Hellhounds don't.

Hellhounds love to see the destruction they can cause in somebody's life, the power and the control they get from upsetting a system or upsetting people. Some people can thrive in an environment like that. Eventually, when you're talking about changing data and embarrassing people in front of others, that positive culture dies—people don't grow, and systems can stay stagnant.

2

Hyena

The Hyena dog personality is an egoistic one. These personalities run in packs of personalities like their own. They are always on the outside of an Alpha lead dog pack. These are the rumor spreaders and mass confusion producers. They will hunt you down together and eat you alive. This dog personality hardly finds the good in others, whether they are his superiors or his juniors in the dog hierarchy. They constantly criticize the efforts of others even if they cannot do better, and if

45

you do not conform to their idea of what is right, they see your methods as trashy.

A Hyena dog may be likened to an examiner who will score students down because they do not answer questions the exact way he wants. It doesn't matter whether they answer the question correctly or not; the examiner has a specific construction of words he expects. If the students give correct answers, but in different forms, the Hyena will not be satisfied.

The narcissistic nature of the Hyena dog makes him believe that his methods are the best, his ways are the best, and even with plausible reasons, he won't apply the methods of other people. The Hyena is usually very arrogant and will show displeasure at your conflicting approaches—even if it will lead to a better or similar end result, it is automatically deemed trash because it is not in line with his method.

If the Hyena dog is the leader of the pack, he will always lay out his hunting plan, explaining every detail, and expecting everyone to be wowed by his idea—even if it isn't that great. He listens to opposing arguments, only to put them in the aside and will ask the whole pack to follow his plan. As a leader, he considers it a weakness to follow his followers' advice and believes that he should be in charge, holding sole control and responsibility of the pack. If they go hunting and a better option surfaces along the line, the Hyena-personality dog will not change his plans. He is very rigid and offers no room for flexibility. He would rather see out his method, even if it fails, than allow his followers to "dictate" what to do for him.

There is no point advising the Hyena dog. It is a fruitless exercise; he is full of himself and will rubbish other ideas. In the rare case where he can see sense in another person's view or opinion, he will initially downplay such method and later fall back to it while claiming full credit for it.

It significantly dampens the self-esteem of the narcissist if he has to succumb to the methods of another; it makes him feel less of a person. Hence, the Hyena dog as a follower is difficult to guide and direct. He always wants to have things his way, making him appear as a rebel, even if he has good intentions.

He is quick to cause divisions among the pack, forming an alliance with weaker dogs, staging divisions, and taking up people to a new pack. The Hyena-personality is never successful with a total coup, as he isn't particularly popular among the pack. Even if he is up against a Hellhound who isn't liked by the pack, his narcissistic nature puts off other people away from him. Hence, Hyenas are only able to convince a small percentage of the pack into their loyal followers.

Although the Hyena dog can poach some of his followers into the new pack, he cannot maintain a sustainable leadership; hence, the dogs that followed him under the new administration will begin to have issues with him. Their interests that aligned at the point of rebellion away from the former pack are never sufficient. The selfish nature of the Hyena will ensure that there is always a conflict of interest—where the Hyena dog's opinion is supreme, no matter how impossible it may seem.

Perhaps one bright side of the Hyena-personality dog is that their narcissistic nature pushes them to work hard, and they are never lazy—even as a leader. They are determined to prove to everyone that their methods are the best and will spare no effort to show that. Hence, they are usually very hardworking.

Stories of the Hyena Dog

The Hyena dog can be found in almost every settlement. It is usually that one person who does not appreciate the efforts of others, always drawing needless comparisons and trying to make people feel bad about themselves. They are never subtle with criticism; they are always point-blank and do not care about the feelings of others when lashing out. They want to quickly make their displeasure known to people once they have conflicting opinions.

In my early twenties, I joined a club with the influence of an older friend, and I was privileged to meet with various people from all walks of life. The club had a sizeable membership of about a hundred people, and more than two-thirds of the members were well-to-do. There were many subsections of friends within the club. As a new member, I only sought to familiarize myself with people, connect with them, and move further in my professional career. In this club, I met different kinds of personalities—it wasn't unexpected anyway, because it was a fellowship involving people from diverse professional and cultural backgrounds across all walks of life.

The president of the club had a Super Alpha personality. He loved everybody equally; he ensured that there was equity in opportunities passed across to members. For instance, if there was a huge contract available to the members of the club, he would award it to the most capable person. However, if there was a smaller contract available, which would seem like a piece of cake to the best person, he would ensure that it was awarded to a developing member, helping the smaller person get bigger. This was the general mode of equity practiced in the club, and it kept away strife from the club—or so it seemed.

There was a distinct subsection of people that particularly caught the eye. They were usually suggesting various policy changes during every meeting, with the opinion that it would be more efficient than the current system. One particular man, Engineer Edwards, was the famous figure in this subsection. He was quite influential and affluent; in fact, he was one of the founding members of the club, having been invited to the club by his former boss when he was much younger.

Engineer Edwards was a person who was well respected by virtue of his longevity in the club. He was quite influential, and he had been of benefit to the club and its members. However, he was known for his narcissism and doggedness. Whenever he made a suggestion that was not followed, he never stopped talking about it and how the club would have been in a better position had his advice been followed. His self-worthiness probably irked people, as he lost consecutive elections to be the president of the club.

Then, he began to gather a set of not-so-loyal loyalists, who were mostly in his subsection. He was fondly supported by one other influential member, Mr. Murphy, who didn't subscribe to the way things were run in the club.

Mr. Murphy was not vocal about his reservations, but once he was happy to stand behind Engineer Edwards and support his opinions, several other less influential members, some of which owed favors to Engineer Edwards, were part of his clique.

As Edwards' sect grew more robust, they began to influence a couple of people who were neither here nor there. With the presence of a few influential people who shared the sentiments of Edwards about needing a different method, they started a new club. Although many people rejected their advances because they were loyal to the leadership of our current club and simply didn't buy into the idea of revolting and being under the leadership of such a narcissist, about 30 percent of the members joined Edwards' new club.

It was quite rosy at the start, as many of the members at Edwards' new club overlooked his constant dismissals of their opinions. The fuzz and euphoria of creating something new overwhelmed them, and they basked in that joy. However, the pleasure was ephemeral, several disagreements began to set in, and Edwards' egoistic nature meant that he was never going to budge for anyone. He didn't run an autocratic system, but his supposed democracy was a farce. Everybody brought their opinions, suggestions, and plans for the new club.

Edwards entertained all opinions, but anyone conflicting with his ideas and methods was ruled over.

He did a lot of hard work in making the Club stand through his methods. Although they were mostly dogged and rigid, his astute dedication ensured success in many ways. Sadly, the success wasn't sustainable. People found themselves too stifled under his leadership and preferred to be in a fellowship where they had the freedom to make decisions and nothing was ever imposed on them. Hence, many began to leave the club. In fact, some old members wanted to return to our club but were too ashamed to come back and instead forfeited membership to both clubs. Eventually, Edwards' leadership style became too unbearable for members. He had a clash of interests with Mr. Murphy and other influential people. The club became heavily divided, and it could no longer afford to continue.

Behind the bloated ego of the Hyena dog lies a very fragile self-esteem that is very vulnerable to criticism. Their arrogance is a defense mechanism against conflicting ideas. If they are in a position where they do not call the shots, they feel very uncomfortable, and easily feel envious of the people in power. Their self-importance is much exaggerated, and they believe that they are as good as anybody else around. Even without any tangible achievements, they want their ideas to be the most recognized, and they want to command a respect that they have not earned. If you have a Hyena-personality dog among your workers, you may need to pay special attention to educate him on the reasons why his ideas are not the best at the moment, or else such a worker will slowly withdraw from making suggestions, looking instead for equally rebellious people who share his sentiment.

A Hyena dog may degenerate into a Hellhound because of his arrogance. He has the tendency to be very violent and aggressive if other people do not budge to his ideologies. It is usually a wide catastrophe if more than one Hyena dog is found in a pack because they are usually at odds, each one wanting to stamp his authority. With leadership positions where they can exert power over people, their narcissism and arrogance make a dreadful combo. From imposing their ideas on people, they become bullies, forcing people to do their wishes. They identify their loyalists and exploit them, and upon the slightest disagreement, they turn on their loyalists. In some communities, these Hyena dogs find themselves in an authoritative leadership position and punish people who do not do things according to their seemingly perfect way. They

are full of themselves, and they consider conflicting ideas as inferior.

3

Super Alpha

The Super Alpha likes to be in charge. When you think of this leader, think about someone who runs for beauty pageants. A politician can also fall into this category. Sometimes this person rises to leadership positions because they look the part. They can give an excellent interview because they prepare and know exactly what to say. He or she adheres to pack rules and is a natural-born leader; they are loyal to their pack to a fault. The problem with their loyalty is that it is hard for them to see the disloyal. Because they are loyal, they refuse to see those who are not because they see themselves as a great leader. Their pride overshadows their thinking.

The Super Alpha always gives the people in their pack the benefit of the doubt; they always give their pack a chance to get themselves back on track, and they never leave a member behind, which is another one of their downfalls. The Super Alpha always has side-kicks; they expect them to be loyal and will overlook any flaws they may have. A Super Alpha will surround himself with his friends rather than those competent in delivering the task that needs to be performed. The Super

Alpha also has a hard time releasing good people when the time comes. He is also always looking to strengthen this pack with quantity and not quality.

A Super Alpha will sacrifice the weak or a just person in the pack to protect his position or the people he likes. When their trust is broken, they will learn from their mistake. If a person crosses them, they will sometimes retaliate, being overbearing and petty. If the Super Alpha cannot trust you, they will be on a mission to remove you from their pack.

This Super Alpha needs to be careful because their strength depends on the inner pack. This can be seen as favoritism and is sometimes unfair to the other pack members. A Super Alpha can turn into a Hellhound if a traumatic event takes place. They can also turn into Hellhounds if there is an uprising in leadership.

The Super Alpha will sometimes engage in forbidden love affairs at work and will mingle business and pleasure at the risk of losing a wonderful job and their integrity.

The Super Alpha will sometimes bully if they feel you are a threat to them being the best. They do have a clique, and it is not always the most knowledgeable people. This puts a glitch in their leadership because instead of strengthening their team with the best people with the best experience or competence, they just want minions to do their bidding. This is fine if the job is mindless in character. However, if the corporation is complex in nature, the Super Alpha's leadership will be flawed to the establishment's detriment.

The Super Alpha is not all flawed because they are great at being the face of a company, being a negotiator, running an LLC, or being a stockbroker.

Super Alpha Stories

I have worked with some wonderful Super Alphas; I even had one come in about once a week to give me a full motivational speech.

This was beneficial to me because I was in the in-crowd; I never condemned the leadership style of this person because the company that I worked at needed a huge morale lift. The company had been deemed unsuccessful for many years—a new transformation was in the works to reconstruct the company. The history of the company had to do with "not keeping enough minorities on the payroll." This becomes important when you are serving a huge minority community. People tend to trust people that look more like them. Although this supervisor had many skill gaps, he was able to keep the people happy and keep the turnovers from happening for some time. Eventually, this person was replaced with a more efficient Alpha; however, this supervisor went on to do other morale lifting types of work.

I have encountered many Super Alphas in the areas of ministry leadership. A leader of this type needs to be empathetic and approachable. But a Super Alpha has to be careful when they're just trying to get people to like them. This can be harmful to the rest of the followers that aren't getting the attention they feel they need. So Super Alphas can definitely have good and bad qualities; however, if they don't mix it with an Alpha's qualities, their personality can backfire on them.

4

The Alpha

Ultimately, the Alpha is the best possible scenario of the dog hierarchy of leadership. An Alpha is a natural-born leader; no matter what they do or where they work, they will always be seen as leaders. This does not mean that they will rise in leadership if they are content and happy with being second in charge. Often, because their leadership is so natural, they are pushed to the front to be a leader. Their gift will usually make room for them at the top.

Some Alphas are happy to be second in command. This way, they don't have all the frustrations or responsibilities of being the head of an organization. The Alphas will mostly adhere to pack rules. They find comfort in following rules and expect others to adhere as well. They include everyone in the group. They try to strengthen the weak but keep a watchful eye on those who are not loyal to the pack. The Alpha is always loyal to whoever their pack leader is. The pack leader usually completely trusts the Alpha.

An Alpha will never try to use their Alpha authority unless the current leader is found to have broken some unpardonable rule. The

Alpha will honestly advise their leader with cautious discretion for the sake of other Alphas in their own positions. The Alpha is usually well-groomed to take over from an Alpha that is moving up or over. The Alpha takes full responsibility if it's their fault in a situation but is not willing to go down with the ship if it is not their fault. The Alpha always gives great warning and discretion to their leader. If their leader seems to be a Super Alpha or Hellhound, the Alpha will put them in place or leave gracefully to find another Alpha position or finally take a leadership role somewhere else. The Alpha always learns from their mistakes and is not quick to anger. This leader watches, listens, and is strategic. He or she will strategically place people in their organization to strengthen it.

The Alpha is not a bully and cannot tolerate bullies. The Alpha will quickly put a Hellhound in their place, but it will not remain under the Hellhound rule. If they do remain under the Hellhound rule, it is because they intend to take complete leadership from the rule of tyranny that a Hellhound produces. The Alpha will not stand by and watch a Hellhound mistreat others in the pack. They are compelled to overrule injustice.

An Alpha can turn into a Hellhound when they take leadership. However, the Alpha tends to grow from their mistakes. A Hellhound will usually be jealous or very watchful of a true Alpha because they know the Alpha carries the full potential to run an organization with the same capability as a Hellhound. The Hellhound is also watchful of the Alpha because the Alpha is a natural-born leader; the pack is drawn to them and that strikes fear into the Hellhound.

5

Beta

People with a Beta personality are usually very adaptable and submissive. They don't really want to be the group's face. Hence they would rather be followers. Due to their high level of productivity, they are usually an asset to any group they find themselves in.

The adaptability of people with a Beta personality makes them open to ideas. They don't usually do things the traditional way, especially if they can discover a better way to achieve the same results, even when things do not go according to plan. Their first instinct is to look for an alternative to achieve their goals; this trait makes them valuable to any group, even when they aren't the leader.

However, their openness to new approaches and methods may be unacceptable to their leader or co-worker, especially if such a person is a Hellhound. The adaptability of these Beta people makes them try out new things for a purpose, and this may be against the normal routine or going against the books. Therefore, their Hellhound boss may term it rebellion and just try to frustrate such a person's efforts.

In my example about my experience with my co-worker, her approach to handling bullies was bullying; as I said, it was weird to me finding out that approach, and many behavior specialists believe that the fear they strike into these kids with bad behavior will shape them. I don't buy into this idea, and I chose a more innovative way of communicating with students that possess that behavior, educating them about why it is bad to bully, giving them examples of why it is bad, listening to them to understand why they bully—in my experience, it is just a coping mechanism some have developed, some want to desperately command respect, and some don't even know it is bad. I could get results with these kids in curbing their bad behaviors without necessarily going through the difficult path as others do. The woman in my workplace saw me as a person threatening her job because of my innovative approach to handling students with miscreant characteristics. While it was typical to mete out punishments for these students to make them know how bad these things were—it didn't always work. As an adaptive specialist, I could develop better ways to achieve this result, and my Hellhound superior felt threatened.

A Beta persona is a person who has an undying quest for knowledge; they are usually not content with little information, as it makes them feel shackled and limited; of course, without knowledge, they can't adequately try out new approaches. Their submissive nature will make them meet even people who are inferior to them for the sake of learning. Unlike Super Alphas and Hellhounds, they do not feel threatened by people with more knowledge; they just want to broaden their horizons. If you pour water from a one-liter cylindrical jar into a one-liter spherical jar, you will achieve the same result. But if you are to pour cubes of sugar from a cylindrical jar into a spherical jar, you may find it difficult to find the same arrangement as before. A Beta persona can be likened to water or liquid because of their adaptability; every situation works for them, unlike the cubes of sugar.

Adaptability is needed in many jobs that require dealing with humans directly, such as marketing, customer service, human resources, and many more. Because humans have different personalities, they cannot be related to in a fixed manner. Adaptability—in this case, flexibility—is important. It is a trait that makes it easy for people to handle transitions in their careers. I had a friend I met on Facebook a few years ago who worked as a factory worker. However, due to the rise in technology, where machines and robots could handle tasks of tens of people to a greater degree of accuracy, he was retrenched. He immediately discovered that the industry was a dying one. The increase of machines bound to continue will cause even more reduced jobs, and another job in the same industry may lead to the same fate in a very short while. So he decided to learn a skill that will not be replaced by machines in a very short while. He began graphics designing.

After learning for a few months after his retrenchment, he offered free cover art suggestions to musicians and filmmakers while pitching his services to several companies. Eventually, he got a remote job with a new company after a year, and he was in charge of all their graphic design work. He constantly improved himself to be in line with the trends. This newly developed skill gave him a bit of freedom, as he could design for other people whenever he had no pressing designs to deliver to the company. In his words, "Even if I get fired again, I can easily get jobs without fear of losing to a machine."

He was a hardworking and productive worker, but he couldn't beat a machine, and he needed to adapt his working environment to prevent that. A person who wasn't adaptive would probably have spent the next couple of months looking for another factory job in the same industry, putting his job security at a huge risk depending on the imminent rise in technology.

People with the Beta persona find it easy to attain happiness and fulfillment; it can be depressing when you try a particular method to solve a problem, but you don't get it done, and then hopelessness sets in for rigid people. However, a Beta dog will just find a way to get a new bone supply and stay happy.

Because adaptable people have a submissive nature, that doesn't really make them take up leadership positions. However, if they do, their adaptable nature allows them to take up dynamic approaches rather than fixed dogmatic ones, ensuring productivity in their team. They are people that ask several questions before making a decision, weighing all options to ensure they aren't rigid. Even if they don't ask other people, they reflect deeply and picture the realities and idealities of all scenarios. With their goal in mind, they go through flexible approaches to get a solution. Their flexibility ensures that they have backup plans in case of unplanned contingencies.

The curiosity of the Beta persona as leaders makes them good listeners; they want to know what everyone on the team has to say, and they believe that everyone has a potential solution to a problem that can be even better than the already laid down plan. The ability to listen makes them bond better with their pack. Like the Alpha dog, which eventually becomes the pack leader, the Beta see themselves as equal with the others and value all opinions with fairness, without an inner clique or favoritism.

This trait, however, can be misinterpreted as a show of weakness, especially from people who have an authoritarian trait like the Super Alphas or the Hellhounds, so they look to usurp the Beta dog and take over the pack. In a professional setting, it will start with the authoritative persona gathering a clique of people who he can influence to stage a coup or organize a takeover of power because the adaptable leader is seen as weak.

Quite interestingly, Beta dogs can also become Hellhounds; constant success in the new approaches they try out can make them feel indispensable, building narcissism in their subconscious. They tend to go out of the norm to find a solution, and their quest for innovativeness can make them rubbish their followers' work because it is seemingly not creative. So they unknowingly crawl into the path of rigidity by seeing themselves as the only person who can think outside the box; hence, they may begin to subsequently shun the opinion of others, invalidating their core principles due to the leadership positions handed to them. Remember that they aren't natural leaders—therefore their submissive nature that gets flipped may lead to a huge sense of narcissism or pride, even without them realizing it.

6

Omega

The Omega persona is typically an insecure one, always looking for validation, endorsement, and encouragement. Although they might be very creative and productive, self-doubt makes them see little worth in themselves and hence unappreciative of their own efforts unless an outsider gives some sort of validation.

They have even worse natural instincts of leadership than someone with a Beta persona.

They are not natural leaders; when found in a professional setting, they are usually alone, desperately trying to avoid situations where they cannot lean on others for help. They most probably will find it difficult to handle a budget proposal because of the fear of questioning. Within them, they think "what if it's wrong," and they would rather avoid the situation.

People like these in a professional setting require a friendly approach to ensure that they don't feel like an outcast. An interested coworker could move away from talking about the work environment to having other casual conversations to make this Omega persona feel free among everyone. The Omega persona sees this act as allegiance and concludes that a person who shows that much empathy won't betray them and hence won't be overly critical with them. They are naturally scared, so reassurance for them is important.

Negative feedback and constructive criticism don't go down well with the Omega dog; they instantly see themselves as a failure. In fact, positive feedback that doesn't explicitly praise them leaves them in doubt; they may feel the positive feedback isn't genuine. If a team leader tells an insecure person "good job," he may feel bad and regard it as damage control for a bad job, whereas it is a good job.

People with the Omega persona need explicit feedback like, "I love the way you handled the files for easy retrieval; I could easily sort out files without having to look at every single one. That was a fantastic job." This kind of compliment feels genuine to people with the Omega persona. In contrast, a person who isn't insecure will have no problems with either compliment or even no compliment as there is a self-assurance of the job done.

Another notable thing about the Omega dog is that they are very conscious of what people will say or think about them. The perception of others matters a lot, and they would not embark on something if it does not give them praises in the court of public opinion, even though the act would have been productive. They would rather do things that will portray them the exact way their immediate audience will appreciate.

Unlike Beta dogs, who want to go outside the rule book to find a new solution, the Omega dog will not want to go against the norm so as not to offend people and would rather stick to the plan cautiously. This makes it really hard for them to improve, and while they may be a bag of talents, the lack of sheer will to take the constructive part of criticism and reevaluate themselves deprives them of improvement.

Although leadership isn't an inherent quality in the Omega dog, they may end up becoming one. They are usually quick to say the most pleasant of things about themselves, even up to their family life; they want their followers to only see the good about them, and while they have weaknesses that can be helped, they would rather leave those weaknesses unaddressed. The only reason they share this information is for public validation, to reassure themselves, and to boost their self-confidence.

They tend to be very nice leaders because they want to be in the good books of everybody; they won't criticize incompetent jobs because they don't want to be seen in a bad light. They would rather avoid talking about the whole situation, in fact. For example, if two co-workers have a disagreement or a very awkward situation at work, rather than address the situation and bring back peace and tranquility, condemning the bad acts, they will allow the situation take a natural course, although it may affect progress at work; they won't talk about it until everything becomes normal again.

Their kindness is a coping mechanism for their insecure nature because they want the tranquility of it. This attribute makes co-workers and junior colleagues have a soft spot for them, seldom challenging them.

In the rare case where the decision of an insecure leader is challenged, they fidget and become very angry as they can't handle criticism. They always want to be right as it fuels their ego and makes them look in control; whereas, people who don't deal with insecurity easily acknowledge that they can't have everything figured out. They emphasize their position, mentioning titles, dismissing better approaches or ideas if it will directly invalidate theirs.

The Omega persona is a weak one, but when found in leadership positions, they don't want to show this weakness. They constantly look over their shoulders, having the mindset that they are being targeted, and they are usually very threatened with more natural and composed leaders even amongst their pack. The potential Alphas, Super Alphas, and or Hellhounds that find themselves under the leadership of this Omega, most likely by hierarchy and duration (especially in a professional setting), usually see through the insensitivity of the Omega dog.

If it starts to harm the pack's progress, there is usually a takeover. This is the Omega dog's fear, but their insecurity even predisposes them more to being deposed. They constantly talk about their positions or rankings, "I am the team leader here; that's why I made that decision." Instead of explaining the reasons for taking certain steps to their pack, they become defensive and feel their authority is challenged, rather than just answering the question for better clarity.

The Omega dog that eventually becomes a leader could evolve into a Hellhound because they don't want authority challenged and they aren't flexible. They shut out intelligent team members who have reasonable contributions because they perceive it as challenging their knowledge, thus reducing productivity and losing valuable employees.

Problems are inevitable, and every leader should know that, but the Omega dog can't handle situations of that sort. They can't celebrate a junior colleague's success because they feel their position is threatened; when an Omega begins to evolve into a Hellhound, he becomes envious of smarter people who are ranks below him, jealousy sets in, and he would rather frustrate such person than celebrate them.

This evolution makes them control freaks, from an employee who never wants to handle public presentations to the boss that doesn't want to entertain conflicting opinions, wanting center stage and wanting to be the center of attention because it feeds their ego. Always attempting to personalize a collective effort, downplaying the impact of others to help their insecurity and make them feel better about themselves. This will harm other workers who value themselves, and gradually, quality will walk out of the door, just like the real-life examples I gave. The Omega persona is probably the one with the worst sense of leadership out of all seven personalities.

7

Delta

The Delta dog is an independent one, a survivor, a one-man army, and has perfected the act of doing things on their own, with little or no communal effort. They understand what is necessary to be done to help themselves, and they will take several risks to do that because they believe they are alone, even when they aren't. People with a Delta persona are usually very skillful because they are used to doing several tasks independently; they learn a lot. They consciously have a relentless quest for knowledge because they understand that the greater their knowledge, the more things they can do on their own. They believe that they are solely responsible for the success, and even if they are in a team, they will not depend on others (even if others can help do a better job in that situation).

When I was in college, I had a very independent classmate, barely went for generally organized tutorials, and didn't participate in any study group. At this time, many of us had study groups. This enabled us to have a better knowledge of what we learned in classes, as a pool of knowledge made it quite easy to learn faster. But my friend, who I will call Ethan in the course of this book, was a renowned loner.

He was very vast; however, he had a good knowledge of all the software used to do group presentations, and during group presentations, he would come up with something for the entire group. In the end, his presentation may be edited to suit other group members' needs, or if the group had something better, Ethan's presentation was ignored. He was typically fine with not receiving help from anybody, and he had good grades. He eventually graduated with a 4.05 GPA in a 5-point grading system. A second-class honors student (upper division) and just 0.45 away from finishing as a first-class graduate.

My course advisor usually told me that "No man is an island; no matter how excellent you are, you need other people to amplify you." Ethan probably would have had better grades in courses where he could have gotten knowledge from others, but he was content with doing things all by himself. In our class of about 60 students, there were a total of five first-class graduates. But the interesting thing was that Ethan was individually better than almost all of them; we knew because of the way he could solve problems nobody else could solve in class, easily impressing all students and lecturers. But he couldn't even finish top five in the class.

Delta dogs can achieve a lot, they have no limit to accumulating knowledge, and they can stand out anywhere; like the Beta dogs, they are highly adaptable. Their adaptability makes it easy for them to open up to new knowledge and approaches, and it gives them flexibility to easily handle many things at a time. Yes, they are great at multitasking. They can effectively manage three huge projects simultaneously with an average of 80% success in all. While the joint effort can produce 95% success, they will singlehandedly produce 80%, which will be well accepted, although it won't be the best that could be achieved.

Their independence makes them not easily swayed by what people say. Unlike the Omega dog, they have a mind of their own. They make decisions based on their belief and pay little attention to external validation as the only validation they regard as important is theirs.

They are usually very responsible people because having to be independent comes with a great deal of responsibility. When you make decisions on your own, you are bound to bear the consequences on your own. Hence, they don't depend on others and hate to appear needy. They will literally explore all available options before asking for help. While this self-reliant attribute is adorable, it is not necessarily the best. They also don't see the need to assist people because they believe that everyone should be responsible. This typically pushes people away from them; like Ethan, they are usually loners.

In social gatherings and parties, they may be very lively and joke around often. Still, once there is no social gathering, they don't want anybody in their space to prevent them from brainstorming independently.

Delta dogs are usually ambitious but very realistic. Because they had to do a lot of things on their own, they know their limits, their strengths, and their shortcomings; this helps them have great self-esteem because they know how much they are worth and won't value themself lesser.

They are natural leaders, as they can handle situations with faltering associates, subordinates, or co-workers. When they have junior colleagues not doing good enough, they just totally ignore them and single-handedly handle the task. But their leadership style is usually flawed because they are usually very poor at carrying the team along—even when the team is filled with brilliant people who can amplify them. They fail to realize that relying on others isn't a sign of weakness but rather a strength.

Teamwork inadvertently brings about better results. If you follow basketball, you will know how good LeBron James is. Individually he is good, but he cannot singlehandedly beat a team of five people, who do not even match up to him, because they are a team; they can help each other's weaknesses. Alpha dogs will ensure all members' participation, leveraging on the best qualities of each dog in the pack to ensure a highly successful effort.

I want to make an example in sports again. In soccer, there are eleven players on each team, divided into attackers, midfielders, defenders, and a goalkeeper. The attackers have the major responsibility of scoring against the opponent, and the defenders alongside the goalkeeper have the major responsibility of preventing a goal from the opponent. If the defenders are not doing their jobs properly, they may lose because their opponent may outscore them, even if their attackers score a few.

Conversely, if the attackers are not scoring on the opponents, then they will not win the match no matter the effort the defenders put in. Defenders and attackers have different qualities, but they are interdependent to achieve a goal. A team that has only attackers, of course, cannot defeat a team that has attackers, midfielders, defenders, and a goal-keeper. Therefore, teamwork lightens the loads of a leader, but the Delta persona refuses to see this.

It may even degenerate to an autocratic leader totally rubbishing his colleagues' opinions if it is not in line with what he has done on his own; this chokes co-workers, and productive associates will eventually leave. Although the Delta persona in leadership could work well initially, as he will inspire others to develop personal skills, in the end, there will be disunity, which will not enable the pack to gather the best available bones.

Conclusion

A leader is only a leader when he has followers. A leader must combine mental skills in line with a personality to ensure that his pack follows his lead. If a person who leads a group of people toward a common goal looks back and the people he is supposedly leading are astray, then there is a defunct in leadership.

Several attributes of various personality types and how they fare in leadership positions have been discussed in earlier chapters, indicating the pros and cons of all attributes, with the

Alpha being the best possible scenario of the dog hierarchy. However, there is at least a good quality from each of the personalities listed above. As a good leader, you should be able to incorporate nearly all into your leadership style. Nobody is perfect, but it is said that you should "aim for the moon—even if you miss, you may land among the stars." So, trying to be close to perfect isn't bad at all.

The very first key to having a loyal pack of followers is communication; when you communicate with your followers, you can easily know what is on their minds. Even if they refuse to talk at the time, your previous communication will enable you to quickly notice the change in attitude. The Alpha dog and the Omega dog are good examples of personas who communicate well. Alphas—because they like to carry everybody along; Omegas—because they seek validation from other people. Either way, it is important to tweak your personality to enable better communication and ensure your pack's loyalty.

Management of manpower, resources, and activities are also good attributes of a leader. Coordination is an admirable trait, and when it is known that you, as a leader of your pack always get things done, your pack will hold you in high esteem. Management is one quality found in Super Alphas; their coordination skills are unmatched, and it serves as an inspiration for their pack.

To effectively lead, it is also important that you can be emulated; your character must not exhibit fear or insecurity as it is a detestable trait. Instead, humility, integrity, and effectiveness in handling tasks are important characters worthy of emulation. When you can be a role model to your followers, your followers will remain loyal, just like the Alpha dogs.

A leader must ensure a good relationship between him and his followers and amongst his followers, unlike the Omega dog that won't settle disputes because he doesn't want to get on the bad side of anybody. A good leader must be able to handle disputes well to ensure harmony; this will ensure the effective completion of tasks, and it will make all followers see that there is no preferential treatment (which is very common in the leadership style of the Super Alpha and the Hellhound). All situations must be judged fairly. A leader must understand every one of his pack, knowing that he should deal with them individually because these attributes in leaders are also found in the followers.

As a good leader, you must be able to deal with individuals in an optimal way to help their productivity. If you have an Omega dog in your pack, you should encourage him frequently, make him partners with a more experienced person, and bring out the creativity in him without being excessively critical. In fact, you can give incentives to some workers to boost their morale and just make them feel good. However, you shouldn't overdo it to avoid the situation appearing as preferential treatment.

Finally, put yourself in your followers' position, and do unto them what you would rather have others do to you. With this leadership guide, you should be able to note your strengths and weaknesses and become an even better leader than you have ever been.

www.ingramcontent.com/pod-product-compliance
Lightning Source LLC
Chambersburg PA
CBHW032149020426
42334CB00016B/1250